D0354418

BRIGHT SHINING

BRIGHT SHINING

One Hope

Messages for Women from

GORDON B. HINCKLEY

DESERET
BOOK

Salt Lake City, Utah

© 2006 40 N. Limited

All rights reserved. No part of this book may be reproduced in any form or by any means without permission in writing from the publisher, Deseret Book Company, P. O. Box 30178, Salt Lake City, Utah 84130. This work is not an official publication of The Church of Jesus Christ of Latter-day Saints. The views expressed herein are the responsibility of the author and do not necessarily represent the position of the Church or of Deseret Book Company.

DESERET BOOK is a registered trademark of Deseret Book Company.

Visit us at deseretbook.com

Library of Congress Cataloging-in-Publication Data

Hinckley, Gordon Bitner, 1910-
  One bright shining hope : messages for women from Gordon B. Hinckley.
    p. cm.
  ISBN-10 1-59038-355-9 (hardbound : alk. paper)
  ISBN-13 978-1-59038-355-1 (hardbound : alk. paper)
1. Mormon women—Religious life. I. Title.
BX8641.H55 2006
248.8′43088289373—dc22

2006021061

Printed in the United States of America
Publishers Printing, Salt Lake City, Utah

10   9   8   7   6   5   4   3   2   1

*I*t is so tremendously important that the women of the Church stand strong and immovable for that which is correct and proper under the plan of the Lord. They must begin in their own homes. They can teach it in their classes. They can voice it in their communities. They must be the teachers and the guardians of their daughters. When you save a girl, you save generations. I see this as the one bright shining hope in a world that is marching toward moral self-destruction.

Of all the creations of the Almighty, there is none more beautiful, none more inspiring than a lovely daughter of God who walks in virtue, with an understanding of why she should do so, who honors and respects her body as a thing sacred and divine, who cultivates her mind and constantly enlarges the horizon of her understanding, who nurtures her spirit with everlasting truth. God will hold us accountable if we neglect His daughters.

My mother died while I was a student in the university. It was a dark and somber day for all of us of that family. But there was a residual that remained with us that gave us strength and guidance and discipline. From her I learned so many things, including respect for womanhood, together with an appreciation for the tremendous strength which she carried within her, including a bright and happy zest for life and a love for people, and incidentally, a tremendously beneficial love for literature, music, and art. From my family life I came to believe, as I still believe, that women have special attributes and qualities. I have come to believe that yours is a godly inheritance.

In the sequence of events as set forth in the scripture, God first created the earth, "and the earth was without form, and void" (Genesis 1:2). He then separated the light from the darkness, and the waters from the land. Then came the creation of vegetation of all kinds, giving the beauty of trees and grass, flowers and shrubs. Then followed the creation of animal life in the sea and upon the land.

Having looked over all of this, He declared it to be good. He then created man in His own likeness and image. Then as His final creation, the crowning of His glorious work, He created woman. I like to regard Eve as His masterpiece after all that had gone before, the final work before He rested from His labors.

I do not regard her as being in second place to Adam. She was placed at his side as an helpmeet. They were together in the Garden, they were expelled together, and they labored together in the world into which they were driven.

Our individual testimonies of these truths are the basis of our faith. We must nurture them. We must cultivate them. We can never forsake them. We can never lay them aside. Without them we have nothing. With them we are everything.

*R*ise to the great potential within you. I do not ask that you reach beyond your capacity. I hope you will not nag yourselves with thoughts of failure. I hope you will not try to set goals far beyond your capacity to achieve. I hope you will simply do what you can do in the best way you know how. If you do so, you will witness miracles come to pass.

I believe this is the best season for women in all the history of the world. In opportunities for education, for the training of your hands and minds, there has never before been a time when doors were so widely opened to you as they are today.

But neither has there been a time, at least in recent history, when you have been confronted with more challenging problems. I need not remind you that the world we are in is a world of turmoil, of shifting values. Shrill voices call out for one thing or another in betrayal of time-tested standards of behavior. The moral moorings of our society have been badly shaken.

I cannot say enough of appreciation for your determination to live by the standards of the Church, to walk with the strength of virtue, to keep your minds above the slough of filth which seems to be moving like a flood across the world. Thank you for knowing there is a better way. Thank you for the will to say no. Thank you for the strength to deny temptation and look beyond and above to the shining light of your eternal potential.

The gospel is a thing of joy. It provides us with a reason for gladness. Of course there are times of sorrow. Of course there are hours of concern and anxiety. We all worry. But the Lord has told us to lift our hearts and rejoice.

We know not what lies ahead of us. We know not what the coming days will bring. We live in a world of uncertainty. For some, there will be great accomplishment. For others, disappointment. For some, much of rejoicing and gladness, good health, and gracious living. For others, perhaps sickness and a measure of sorrow. We do not know. But one thing we do know. Like the polar star in the heavens, regardless of what the future holds, there stands the Redeemer of the world, the Son of God, certain and sure as the anchor of our immortal lives. He is the rock of our salvation, our strength, our comfort, the very focus of our faith.

God bless you, mothers. When all the victories and defeats of men's efforts are tallied, when the dust of life's battles begins to settle, when all for which we labor so hard in this world of conquest fades before our eyes, you will be there, you must be there, as the strength for a new generation, the ever-improving onward movement of the race.

experienced times of discouragement on my mission, as does every missionary. On an occasion or two, when the clouds were particularly dark, I felt in a very real but indescribable way the protecting, guiding, encouraging influence of my mother. She seemed very close. I tried then, as I have tried since, to so conduct my life and perform my duty as to bring honor to her name.

There is nothing in all this world as magnificent as virtue. It glows without tarnish. It is precious and beautiful. It is above price. It cannot be bought or sold. It is the fruit of self-mastery.

"Let virtue garnish thy thoughts unceasingly."

(D&C 121:45)

23

I have discovered that life is not a series of great heroic acts. Life at its best is a matter of consistent goodness and decency, doing without fanfare that which needed to be done when it needed to be done. I have observed that it is not the geniuses that make the difference in this world. I have observed that the work of the world is done largely by men and women of ordinary talent who have worked in an extraordinary manner.

We honor best those who

have gone before when we serve

well in the cause of truth.

You are very precious, each of you, regardless of your circumstances. You occupy a high and sacred place in the eternal plan of God, our Father in Heaven. You are His daughters, precious to Him, loved by Him, and very important to Him. His grand design cannot succeed without you.

I wish with all of my heart that every marriage might be a happy marriage. I wish that every marriage might be an eternal partnership. I believe that wish can be realized if there is a willingness to make the effort to bring it to pass. God bless you, my beloved sisters, who stand as the queens in your home, that you may be happy with that happiness which comes of the knowledge that you are loved and honored and treasured.

*M*ay I suggest that you walk with prayer and faith, with charity and love. Our Father in Heaven has endowed His daughters with a unique and wonderful capacity to reach out to those in distress, to bring comfort and succor, to bind up the wounds and heal the aching heart.

*M*arvelous is the power of women of faith. It has been demonstrated again and again in the history of this church. It goes on among us today. I think it is part of the divinity within you.

Sisters, rise to the stature of that divinity. In that effort make the world in which you live a better place for yourself and for all who will come after you. There is much to do. There are many challenges to be met.

I have often thought that if great numbers of the women of all nations were to unite and lift their voices in the cause of peace, there would develop a worldwide will for peace which could save our civilization and avoid untold suffering, misery, plague, starvation, and the death of millions.

In the pioneering days of this church when men grubbed the sagebrush and broke the sod so that crops might be planted to sustain life, many a wife and mother planted a few flowers and a few fruit trees to add beauty and taste to the drabness of pioneer life. There are so many things that you can do. Beauty is a thing divine. The cultivation of it becomes an expression of the divine nature within you.

Every woman has as certain a right to approach the throne of deity in prayer as does any man. I am convinced that our Father in Heaven loves His daughters as much as He loves His sons and that He is as ready to hear their pleas and grant their petitions.

The things of God are understood by the Spirit of God. That Spirit is real. To those who have experienced its workings, the knowledge so gained is as real as that received through the operation of the five senses.

*N*o woman can afford to demean herself, to belittle herself, to downgrade her abilities or her capacities. Let each be faithful to the great, divine attributes that are within her. Be faithful to the gospel. Be faithful to the Church.

To you women of today, who are old or young, may I suggest that you write, that you keep journals, that you express your thoughts on paper. Writing is a great discipline. It is a tremendous education effort. It will assist you in various ways, and you will bless the lives of many—now and in the years to come, as you put on paper some of your experiences and some of your musings.

*C*ultivate an attitude of happiness. Cultivate a spirit of optimism. Walk with faith, rejoicing in the beauties of nature, in the goodness of those you love, in the testimony which you carry in your heart concerning things divine.

He who is our Eternal Father has blessed you with miraculous powers of mind and body. He never intended that you should be less than the crowning glory of His creations.

*T*rain your minds and your hands that you may be equipped to serve well in the society of which you are a part. Cultivate the art of being kind, of being thoughtful, of being helpful. Refine within you the quality of mercy, which comes as a part of the divine attributes you have inherited.

You need never feel inferior. You need never feel that you were born without talents or without opportunities to give them expression. Cultivate whatever talents you have, and they will grow and refine and become an expression of your true self appreciated by others.

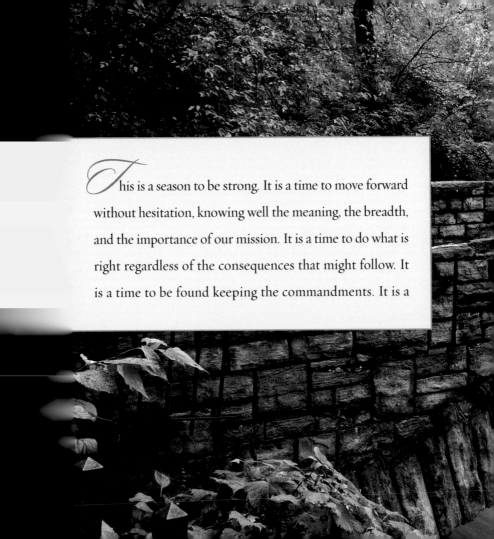

*T*his is a season to be strong. It is a time to move forward without hesitation, knowing well the meaning, the breadth, and the importance of our mission. It is a time to do what is right regardless of the consequences that might follow. It is a time to be found keeping the commandments. It is a

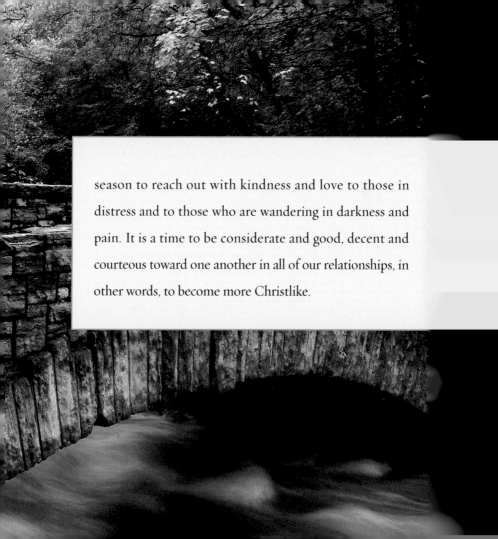

season to reach out with kindness and love to those in distress and to those who are wandering in darkness and pain. It is a time to be considerate and good, decent and courteous toward one another in all of our relationships, in other words, to become more Christlike.

Each of us can do a little better than we have been doing. We can be a little more kind. We can be a little more merciful. We can be a little more forgiving. We can put behind us our weaknesses of the past and go forth with new energy and increased resolution to improve the world about us, in our homes, in our places of employment, in our social activities.

*N*ever lose faith in your opportunity to lift those
who are in need, to give strength to those who are weak,
to give encouragement to those who falter by the way.

am satisfied that every man or woman who goes to the temple in a spirit of sincerity and faith leaves the house of the Lord a better man or woman. There is need for constant improvement in all of our lives. There is need occasionally to leave the noise and the tumult of the world and step within the walls of a sacred house of God, there to feel His Spirit in an environment of holiness and peace.

$\mathcal{R}$each out to help one another. All of us need help from time to time. We need encouragement. We need friends who will stand by us through thick and thin. I ask each of you to be that kind of a friend.

No other work reaches so close

to divinity as does the nurturing of

the sons and daughters of God.

Let us be true disciples of the Christ, observing the Golden Rule, doing unto others as we would have them do unto us. Let us strengthen our own faith and that of our children while being gracious to those who are not of our faith. Love and respect will overcome every element of animosity. Our kindness may be the most persuasive argument for that which we believe.

T am no longer a young man filled with energy and vitality. I am an old man. I'm given to meditation and prayer. I would enjoy sitting in a rocker, swallowing prescriptions, listening to soft music, and contemplating the things of the universe. But such activity offers no challenge and makes no contribution.

I wish to be up and doing. I wish to face each day with resolution and purpose. I wish to use every waking hour to give encouragement, to bless those whose burdens are heavy, to build faith and strength of testimony.

I believe our problems, almost every one, arise out of the homes of the people. If there is to be reformation, if there is to be a change, if there is to be a return to old and sacred values, it must begin in the home. It is here that truth is learned, that integrity is cultivated, that self-discipline is instilled, and that love is nurtured.

*N*o matter where we are, no matter our circumstances, we all can be faithful Latter-day Saints. We can pray and worship the Lord in the privacy of our own closet. We can sing anthems of praise to the Almighty even when we are alone. We can study the scriptures. We can live the gospel. We can pay our tithes and offerings though the amount be ever so small. We can walk in faith. We can strive to live lives patterned after the life of our Master.

Why are we such a happy people? It is because of our faith, the quiet assurance that abides in our hearts that our Father in Heaven, overseeing all, will look after His sons and daughters who walk before Him with love and appreciation and obedience.

We need to build and strengthen one another. We must never lose sight of the fact that we are to "succor the weak, lift up the hands which hang down, and strengthen the feeble knees" (D&C 81:5).

Great are our blessings. Tremendous is our responsibility. Let us get on our knees and plead with the Lord for direction. Then let us stand on our feet, square up our shoulders, and march forward without fear to enlarge among people everywhere the righteousness of the Lord.

$\mathcal{G}$iven what we have and what we know, we ought to be a better people than we are. We ought to be more Christlike, more forgiving, more helpful and considerate to all around us.

I've said to missionaries many times, in a rather joking way, as I have met with them, "Are you the kind of missionary your mother thinks you are? Are you the kind of son or daughter your mother thinks you are?" You know, if we would be the kind of boys and girls, sons and daughters, our mothers think we are, we'd all be pretty good.

People ask me what is my favorite scripture. I tell them I have a number of them. One of them is this great statement found in the 50th section of the Doctrine and Covenants: "That which is of God is light; and he that receiveth light, and continueth in God, receiveth more light; and that light groweth brighter and brighter until the perfect day" (D&C 50:24). That, to me, is a great, basic, marvelous, wonderful truth.

$\mathcal{I}$ have been asked, "What is your most important accomplishment in life?" Oh, I do not know. We have had failures and accomplishments. We are like you. We are just garden-variety people who go along trying to do what is expected of us and do it in a way that the Lord would have us do it. I do not know that there is one great accomplishment that stands out in my life. I have just tried to do what I felt was right and give my strength and energy moving forward the work of the Lord while trying along the way to bless the lives of other people.

Cultivate in your hearts a testimony and a love for God your Eternal Father. We sing, "I am a child of God" (*Hymns,* no. 301). That isn't just a figment, a poetic figment—that is the living truth. There is something of divinity within each of us that needs cultivation, that needs to come to the surface, that needs to find expression. You fathers and mothers, teach your children that they are, in a very literal way, sons and daughters of God. There is no greater truth in all the world than that—to think that we have something of divinity in us.

In a very large measure each of us holds the key to the blessings of the Almighty upon us. If we wish the blessing, we must pay the price. A part of that price lies in being faithful. Faithful to what? Faithful to ourselves, to the very best that is within us.

*L*et me say to you sisters that you do not hold a second place in our Father's plan for the eternal happiness and well-being of His children. You are an absolutely essential part of that plan.

Each of you is a daughter of God, endowed with divine birthright. You need no defense of that position.

*I*s there anything more beautiful, anything that speaks more of divinity than a lovely little girl? I have little great-granddaughters, bright-eyed and beautiful, who sing and smile and touch my heart with thoughts of heaven. When I see them in their innocence, I recall the words of the Lord, "Except ye . . . become as little children, ye shall not enter into the kingdom of heaven" (Matthew 18:3).

I can remember when I was a small boy, five years old, President Joseph F. Smith announced to all the Church that they should gather their families together in family home evening. My father said, "The President of the Church has asked that we do it, and we are going to do it."

So we all gathered in family home evening. It was funny. He said, "We'll sing a song." Well, we were not singers. We just tried to sing and laughed at one another. So we did with a lot of other things. But out of that experience there gradually came something that was wonderful—a practice that helped us, that drew us together as a family, that strengthened us, and there grew in our hearts a conviction of the value of family home evening. I have practiced that in my home. My children have practiced it in their homes. They now have sons and daughters who practice it in their homes. And that is the way it goes.

We have a tremendous responsibility. I do not hesitate to say that. So much depends on us. If not me, who? If not now, when? It is our job here and now to do our best to make a difference.

*W*e have a hymn that we sing in our meetings:

When upon life's billows you are tempest-tossed,

When you are discouraged, thinking all is lost,

Count your many blessings; name them one by one,

And it will surprise you what the Lord has done.

("Count Your Blessings," *Hymns,* no. 241)

In times of darkness, try to get to the house of the Lord and there shut out the world. Receive His holy ordinances, and extend these to your forebears. At the conclusion of a session in the temple, sit quietly in the celestial room and ponder the blessings you have received in your own behalf or that you have extended to those who have gone beyond. Your heart will swell with gratitude, and thoughts of the eternal verities of the Lord's great plan of happiness will infuse your soul.

*B*elieve in yourself. Believe in your capacity to do great and good things. Believe that no mountain is so high that you cannot climb it. Believe that no storm is so great that you cannot weather it. You are not destined to be a scrub. You are a child of God, of infinite capacity.

Believe that you can do it—whatever it is that you set your heart on. Opportunities will unfold and open before you. The skies will clear when they have been dark with portent.

As I look back upon my life and think of the wonder of the companion who walked so long beside me, I cannot get over the tremendous influence that she had on me. She was the mother of my children. She gave them life. She nurtured them. She guided them through their formative years. She loved them and dreamed of them and prayed for them.

She was so wise and good. She just seemed to have present in her all the good qualities of her most sterling forebears. All of these seemed to come together in that one little girl who bewitched me when I was young and in love.

Now a beautiful marker of enduring granite marks her final resting place, and engraved in that stone, beneath her name, are the words, "Beloved Eternal Companion."

And so she will be mine and I will be hers through all of the eternities to come.

*A*ccept every responsibility that you are given, and execute it with faith and diligence. The Lord will bless you. He will magnify you. Your life will be the richer, your experience the sweeter because of your service. This church is not man's creation. It is man's opportunity afforded him by his Maker. It is eternal in its nature, in its doctrine, in its program.

> *True to the faith that our parents have cherished,*
> *True to the truth for which martyrs have perished,*
> *To God's command,*
> *Soul, heart, and hand,*
> *Faithful and true we will ever stand.*
>
> ("True to the Faith," *Hymns*, no. 254)

People wonder what we do

for our women. I tell you what

we do: we get out of their way

and look with wonder at what

they are accomplishing.

*R*ead the scriptures to your children. You may not think they understand. They won't understand everything you read. But they will develop within themselves a feeling, an attitude, a spirit that will be wonderful. And I don't hesitate to promise you that the day will come, if you nurture your children and love and teach in righteousness, you will get on your knees with tears in your eyes and thank the Lord for His blessing you.

I hope for you the very best that life has to offer, but I hope even more for a few simple things—things that come of heart, things that come of the spirit, things that come of the divine within each of us.

When all is said and done, when you have lived your life and grown as old as I am, you will recognize that it is the simple virtues that count, that make the great differences in our lives. It is better to sleep at night with a clear conscience than to worry oneself sick while living a fraud.

When all is said and done, our success in life will not be spelled out in the money we make, in the honors we attain, in the plaudits of men, but in those virtues which become the essence of that which is greatest within each of us.

The world needs the touch of women and their love, their comfort, and their strength. Our harsh environment needs their encouraging voices, the beauty that seems to fall within their natures, the spirit of charity that is their inheritance. The God in whom so many of us believe has endowed His daughters with a unique and wonderful capacity to reach out to those in distress, to bring comfort and succor, to bind up wounds and heal aching hearts, and, most of all, to rear children with love and understanding.

*S*tand tall and be strong in defense of those great virtues which have been the backbone of our social progress. When you are united, your power is limitless. You can accomplish anything you wish to accomplish. And oh, how very, very great is the need for you in a world of crumbling values where the adversary seems so very much to be in control.

*N*one of us is wise enough to make it on our own. We need the help, the wisdom, the guidance of the Almighty in reaching those decisions that are so tremendously important in our lives. There is no substitute for prayer. There is no greater resource.

You have nothing in this world more precious than your children. When you grow old, when your hair turns white and your body grows weary, when you are prone to sit in a rocker and meditate on the things of your life, nothing will be so important as the question of how your children have turned out. It will not be the money you have made. It will not be the cars you have owned. It will not be the large house in which you live. The searing question that will cross your mind again and again will be "How well have my children done?"

*I*t's been the mothers who have been the great carriers and purveyors of faith throughout the history of this Church. I believe that with all my heart.

May I express my gratitude to you faithful Latter-day Saint women, now numbered in the millions and found across the earth. Great is your power for good. Marvelous are your talents and devotion. Tremendous is your faith and your love for the Lord, for His work, and for His sons and daughters. Continue to live the gospel. Magnify it before all of your associates. Your good works will carry more weight than any words you might speak. Walk in virtue and truth, with faith and faithfulness. You are part of an eternal plan, a plan designed by God our Eternal Father. Each day is a part of that eternity.

Are these perilous times?

They are. But there is no need to fear.

We can have peace in our hearts

and peace in our homes. We can be an

influence for good in this world,

every one of us.

*L*et us be a happy people. The Lord's plan is a plan of happiness. The way will be lighter, the worries will be fewer, the confrontations will be less difficult if we cultivate a spirit of happiness.

The true strength that is America's, the true strength of any nation, lies in those qualities of character that have been acquired for the most part by children taught in the quiet, simple, everyday manner of mothers. What Jean Paul Richter once declared of fathers is even more true of mothers—and I paraphrase it just a little to make the point—"What a mother says to her children is not heard by the world, but it will be heard by posterity."

Pray for wisdom and understanding as you walk the difficult paths of your lives. If you are determined to do foolish and imprudent things, I think the Lord will not prevent you. But if you seek His wisdom and follow the counsel of the impressions that come to you, I am confident that you will be blessed.

Someone has said,

"Be kind to the women. They

constitute half of the population and

are mothers to the other half."

You are doing the best you can, and that best results in good to yourself and to others. Do not nag yourself with a sense of failure. Get on your knees and ask for the blessings of the Lord; then stand on your feet and do what you are asked to do.

Life is never a failure until we call it such. There are so many who need your helping hands, your loving smile, your tender thoughtfulness.

In His grand design, when God first created man, He created a duality of the sexes. The ennobling expression of that duality is found in marriage. One individual is complementary to the other. As Paul stated, "Neither is the man without the woman, neither the woman without the man, in the Lord" (1 Corinthians 11:11). There is no other arrangement that meets the divine purposes of the Almighty. Man and woman are His creations. Their duality is His design. Their complementary relationships and functions are fundamental to His purposes. One is incomplete without the other.

I come to you with a plea that we stop seeking out the storms and enjoy more fully the sunlight. I am suggesting that as we go through life we try to "accentuate the positive." I am asking that we look a little deeper for good, that we still our voices of insult and sarcasm, that we more generously compliment virtue and effort.

*T*he right to receive the temple ordinances pertains as much to women as it does to men. The blessings to be received through that experience are as great for women as they are for men.

As you walk your various paths,
walk with faith. Speak affirmatively
and cultivate an attitude of confidence. You
have the capacity to do so. Your strength
will give strength to others.

Some years ago I clipped an article on Commander William Robert Anderson, the man who first took a submarine under the North Pole from the waters of the Pacific to the waters of the Atlantic. It was an untried and dangerous mission. In his wallet he carried a tattered card with these words: "I believe I am always divinely guided, I believe I will always take the right road, I believe God will always make a way where there is no way" (in Christopher S. Wren, "If It's 3-to-1 against Anderson: Can a Congressman Afford a Conscience?" *Look*, April 20, 1971, 48).

"Be not afraid, only believe."

(Mark 5:36)

You did not come into the world to fail. You came into the world to succeed. You have accomplished much so far. It is only the beginning. As you move forward on the trail of life, keep the banner of faith in self ever before you. You may not be a genius. You may not be exceptionally smart. But you can be good, and you can try. And you will be amazed at what might happen when in faith you take a step forward.

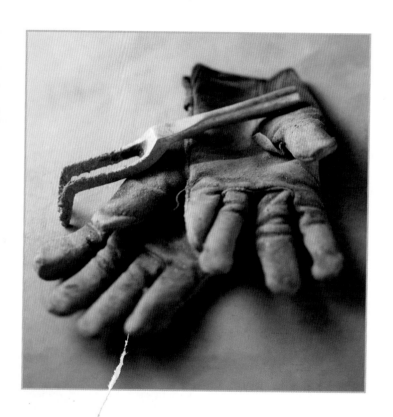

*M*ay the Lord bless you, my beloved sisters. You are the guardians of the hearth. May you be strengthened for the challenges of the day. May you be endowed with wisdom beyond your own in dealing with the problems you constantly face. May your prayers and your pleadings be answered with blessings upon your heads and upon the heads of your loved ones.